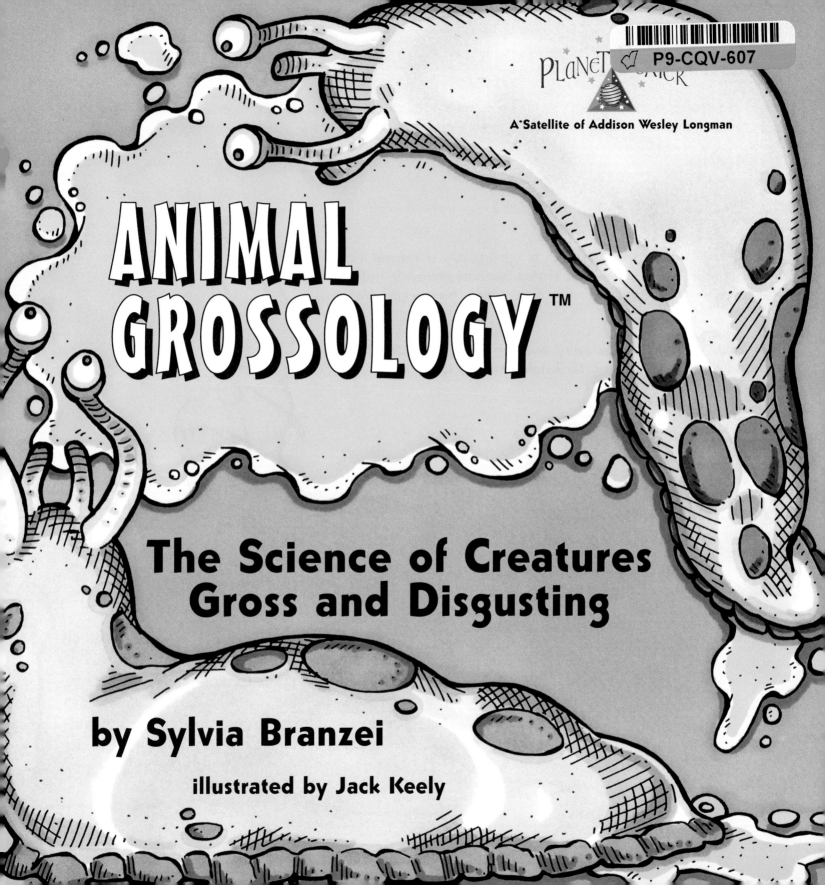

PLANET DEXTER

A Satellite of Addison Wesley Longman

ANIMAL GROSSOLOGY™

The Science of Creatures Gross and Disgusting

by Sylvia Branzei

illustrated by Jack Keely

ISBN 0-201-95994-1

This book is dedicated to every budding grossologist and to my sisters, Kris, Gloria, and Aleis, for helping me and loving me.

Cover design by C. Shane Sykes
Interior design by C. Shane Sykes and Jack Keely
Illustrated by Jack Keely

Set in various sizes of Grizzly, Gill Sans, and Mister Earl.

1 2 3 4 5 6 7 8 9 -GC- 0099989796
First printing, September 1996

Through the Addison Wesley Longman TRI△NGLE Program, Planet Dexter books are available FROM YOUR BOOKSELLER at special discounts for bulk purchases; or contact the Corporate, Government, and Special Sales Department at Addison Wesley Longman, One Jacob Way, Reading, MA 01867; or call (800) 238-9682.

AND NOW A MESSAGE FROM OUR CORPORATE LAWYER:

"Neither the Publisher nor the Author shall be liable for any damage that may be caused or sustained as a result of conducting any of the activities in this book without specifically following instructions, conducting the activities without proper supervision, or ignoring the cautions contained in the book."

Animal Grosstents

A Gross Introduction

"You won't believe the disgusting creatures I saw."

"Yeah, tell me. I've seen some pretty strange things."

"Well, for starters, they're really big. At least 10 times bigger than we are. And they're almost hairless. Yep, just skin all over the place except for a few blotches in certain places. And in those places there is a *lot* of hair."

"Sounds awful."

"That's just the beginning. They poop and pee in a special spot, which is OK, until you find out that they share the same spot. Really. One will go in the spot, and then another will even wait to go in the exact same spot." **"Yuck!"**

"They stink something awful and they know it. Sweat seeps from all over their bodies, so they rub stuff like wax, plants, ashes, and fat on themselves to cover the smell. Sometimes the rubbing stuff makes them smell even worse."

"Wow, I can't wait to tell my cousins."

"Oh no! Here comes one now!

They can be quite ferocious.

I'm outta here."

"Yeah, let's go."

4

If animals could talk, they would probably discuss the strange and disgusting ways of humans. But they can't so it is we who say things like "Yuck, a slug" (*squash*), and "Gross, a bug" (*squish*). If animals could read and write, they might publish whole books about how gross humans are. But they can't, so this book will concentrate on only those creatures that truly rank as disgusting from a human viewpoint. **Leeches. Slugs. Lice. Slime Molds. Humans**.

Hey, you included humans in that list—

As a budding Grossologist, you will soon begin to call them as you see them.

Don't Be a Slime Mold! Don't Be a Hagfish!

Since you're a human, make the most of having an opposable thumb: pick up a pen and write to us! Tell us what you think of this gross book. Here's what to put on the envelope:

The Editors of Planet Dexter
One Jacob Way
Reading, MA 01867

Or fax us at 617-944-8243. Or zap us a line at pdexter@aw.com. When we recover from being so grossed out (and that could take a very long time, so be patient), we just might write you back.

Vomit Munchers

Here comes breakfast!

Rrrraaaaallllllfffff.

After you hurl, you probably don't go running for a spoon. **"Yuck!"**

But for some animals, vomit is a way of life. The leader of the vomit munchers is the common housefly.

Hey, I just shooed one away from my sandwich!

It probably left vomit on your sandwich after it had a taste. *Ack!*

Barf, suck, barf, suck.

Imagine what it would be like if you ate only vomit. Although it sounds unpleasant, without constant puke action a housefly would not survive. It would starve.

A fly travels about in search of fly excitement. (For a fly, excitement is tasty food treats.) The fly stops here and there to taste with its feet.

Bzzzzzzbzzzzz. Stop. Step. Taste.

Nope.

Bzzzzzzbzzzzz. Stop. Step. Taste.

Yummmmm, a chocolate chip cookie.

Your chocolate chip cookie is waiting for you to finish your cheese sandwich. The fly finds a sweet bit, hurls on your cookie, then uses its spongelike tongue to mop up the barf cookie soup. You finish your cheese sandwich. The fly completes its barfy cookie treat and takes off. You bite into your chocolate-chip-and-fly-barf cookie. "This cookie tastes even better than usual. I wonder why it tastes different?"

Flies don't try to be rude eaters. It's just that they don't have any teeth, sucking tubes, or biting mouth parts. Flies live on a liquid diet. When a fly comes across a yummy solid treat, it retches stomach digestive juices on to the food. The digestive chemicals dissolve the solid food and turn it into liquid. The fly mops up the liquid with its tongue.

This really wouldn't be so bad if they didn't have such sticky feet. *Sticky feet?* The feet have claws and sticky pads. For strolling on the counter, the fly uses the claws. The sticky pads are reserved for the great walking-on-the-ceiling trick. Behind each claw are hairs that drip gluey liquid. The fly squirts the sticky stuff, then pulls out its foot when it wants to walk. When it moves the gummy foot, freeloaders (germs) come along for the ride. One scientific study had a fly stroll around a gelatin plate. After several days, little white trails formed along the fly's path. The white trails were made of growing bacteria.

Actually, the sticky feet aren't so bad, if flies didn't also have hairy legs. *Hairy legs?* Flies taste with their feet and legs. Little hairs on their legs and feet act like human tongues. A fly lands on a dead bird. The little hairs brush the surface. If the surface seems edible, the flies mouth tube goes into barf action.

"All right! Pigeon for dinner."

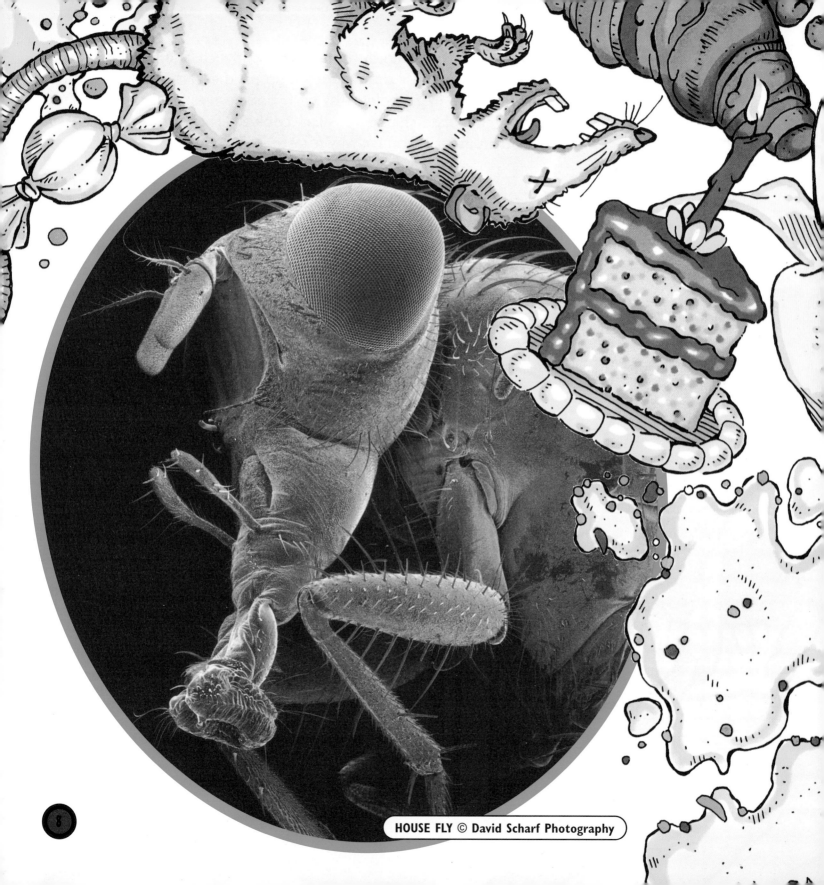

8

Maybe you've watched a housefly flit from spot to spot, tasting its way along your kitchen table. Often it stops to feed in spots with sugar sprinkles. This is because the hairy taste organs are very sensitive to sugar. Guess you could say that flies have a real sweet foot. The little hairs also pick up disgusting stuff, such as bacteria and other germs. Sticky feet and hairy legs aren't the problem though. The real problem is that flies are not picky eaters. A fly may travel almost 15 miles over several days, tasting all the way.

B$_{ZZZZZ}$B$_{ZZZZZ}$. **A banana, yumm, barf, suck.**

B$_{ZZZZZ}$B$_{ZZZZZ}$. **Cow dookie, yes, ralf, lap.**

B$_{ZZZZZ}$B$_{ZZZZZ}$. **Rotting dead rat, vomit, smack, smack.**

B$_{ZZZZZ}$B$_{ZZZZZ}$. **My favorite: birthday cake, hurl, sip.**

"Shoo fly. Get off of my birthday cake. Anyone want another slice?"

A study of 414 houseflies found an average of 1,250,000 bacteria on a typical fly body. When a fly lands in your soup, you can't be sure where that thing has been, or what it has eaten. The sticky pads and legs may be coated with numerous critters. Also, when the fly vomits, it spits out some of the leftover food from the last meal. What if that last meal was dog poop? **Yuck, indeed.**

Most of the fly freeloaders are harmless, but most isn't all. To make sure you don't get sick from fly yuck:

- **Cover food or don't leave it out during fly season.**
- **Clean up any dookie that may attract flies.**
- **Put screens on your doors and windows.**
- **Clean up any garbage around your house or yard.**
- **If a fly lands on your food, remove the spot where the fly tasted, and throw it away.**

Hornets eat houseflies. Some American settlers hung hornets' nests in their homes to get rid of the flies.

PENGUINS © M. Phil Kahl/DRK Photo

At least that's how it works if you're a baby penguin.

Many loving mommy and daddy birds, such as doves, finches, and herons, vomit into their hungry babies' mouths. Others, such as gulls, spew all over the floor of the nest and the babies pick at the food. No need to clean up the mess.

Baby bird food is stuff that the parent ate but did not completely digest. The scientific word for puking up undigested food is **regurgitation (ree gurge e TAY shun)**. Actually, the barf meal doesn't come from the stomach at all. When the parent bird swallows the food, it goes down the throat and into a storage sack called the **crop**. At the nest, the food comes out of storage. Pretty good trick, if you don't have cupboards or pantries to keep stuff in.

This disgusting act of parental care works great for birds. Baby birds chow a lot. They can eat up to their full weight in food every day. A bird that regurgitates to its young makes less trips than a bird that brings actual food items. So, some barf in the crop is better than two worms in the mouth. Also, it is easier for the parent birds to share amongst their young a puke meal than to share a cricket. When the baby birds are grown, the parents stop providing the barf food.

"Remember when we were young, mom and dad used to spew that great worm puke?

I really miss that."

Seagulls have a red dot on their beaks. When a baby gull is hungry, it pecks on the red spot. This causes the parent to open its mouth and hurl out the young's dinner.

11

CUD CUD CUD CUD CUD CUD

"SO, WHAT ARE YOU UP TO?"

"OH, JUST SITTING AROUND CHEWING THE CUD."

Yep, that's the life of a cow. Actually, it is also the life of goats, camel, deer, antelope, and sheep. Eat, upchuck, chew the barfed up cud. About nine hours of every cow day is spent chewing cud.

Cud is great stuff. The cud muncher, or **ruminant (ROO ma nent)**, packs away food for snacking later. No need to travel to quickie mart for a late night snack, just spit up some cud and munch. Convenience is not why ruminants chew cud. The real reason is that they cannot digest food any other way. Cud chewers are grazing animals. That means they eat mostly grasses. If their stomachs were like human bellies, they could not break down the grasses, so they would suffer from constant stomach aches. They get around this problem by having divided stomachs.

A cow has one stomach but it is in four parts. In all ruminants, the first part of the stomach is called the **rumen (ROO men)**. The cow grabs a hunk of grass and swallows it. The rule of "chew your food well before swallowing" does not apply.

The wad of grass goes into the cow's rumen. This part of the stomach is packed full of wee critters called bacteria and protozoa. In each drop of cow rumen juice about 10,000,000,000 microcreatures live. There are more critters in one drop of rumen liquid than there are people living on Earth. These microanimals digest the fiber in grass for the cow or goat or whatever. For their work, the rumen creatures get sugar and protein from the grass. Vinegar and other acids form as the bacteria munch on the grasses. Basically, the bacteria kind of pickle and warm the grass to form a yummy pickled grass stew.

One type of gut bacteria also produces a lot of methane gas, which makes cows and other ruminants belch and fart a lot.

For the cud munchers, you could say, "What goes down, must come up." Several hours after chewing the cud patty, the cow heaves up the grass mush wad mixed with a lot of wee beasties for a second flavor event. The cud lump is also call a **bolus (BOW less)**.

BURP

A cow's stomach is equal in size to nine human stomachs.

Now the real chewing begins. The bolus is mixed with saliva. Humans make about one liter of saliva each day. A sheep or goat tops humans, with up to 15 liters per day. Coming in first by producing almost 200 liters of daily saliva—the cow. The saliva helps to break down the bolus. A saliva chemical takes away some of the acids in the cud concoction.

The completely chewed cud is reswallowed. Now the mash is sent to another stomach pouch where chemicals digest the twice-eaten food. The chemicals also digest the microcreatures that went along for the bolus. These creatures are actually an important part of the cud chewers' diet. The digestion map is now similar to that of all animals: stomach to intestine to colon to anus to . . .

plop!

To help them digest wood, termites also have microcreatures in their stomachs. Termites fart a lot due to the methane produced by the little gut friends.

Yep, termites have flatulence.

15

Try this on someone who thinks she knows a lot.

Get a piece of paper and ask the volunteer to draw an animal from the following description. "It has no head or brain. Most animals of this kind have five or more arms, but no fingers. Attached to the bottom of each arm are feet, no legs. The feet are usually in pairs, and one animal can have over 1,000 feet. In the center of the feet is this animal's toothless mouth. This animal is often covered with bumps or little spines. It comes in various colors, such as purple, red, and yellow."

You'll probably get really strange drawings. But you've just described sea stars perfectly.

Sea stars live in all the oceans of the world. *Sea stars?* The more scientific name for starfish is **sea star**. Most sea stars look like the little five-pointed stars that you draw on pictures of the night sky. The five points are the arms of the sea star. The part in the middle of the arms is the body. Under the arms are rows of feet. Yep, no legs. A sea star can have as many as 1,200 little feet.

The feet don't have toes or paws; instead, they are shaped like tubes with suction cups at the end. The sucker feet help sea stars get a grip. Sea stars are pretty weird.

All of this is very interesting, but what about sea star vomit?

Basically, the sea star eats by regurgitating in an odd way. This ocean creature shoves its stomach out its mouth, digests the food, then sucks the stomach back in. Kind of like barfing backward. Imagine if that were how humans ate!

The sea star wanders around the ocean bottom looking for other animals to eat. If it finds a clam, it wraps its legs around the shell. The suction feet attach to the clam and pull. Talk about a bear hug. The sea star needs to open the shell only a tiny bit; a slit as thin as the edge of one page of this book is enough. Then the hungry beast upchucks its stomach into the opening. Once inside, the stomach releases chemicals that digest the soft body in the shell. After the body is liquidy, the sea star sucks the barf dinner along with the stomach back into its mouth.

Do you think sea stars burp after a big meal?

Seal poops is a chosen food for one type of Antarctic sea star.

When attacked, some sea stars lose or throw off an arm or two, then grow new ones later. Before humans understood this, clam and oyster harvesters cut sea stars into pieces and threw them back into the ocean. They thought they would get rid of the sea star pests this way. Instead, the sea star pieces became new sea stars and a huge population explosion occurred.

Some animals are natural pukers rather than vomit munchers.

Unlike vomit munchers, natural pukers don't eat barf, they just spew regularly. Humans do it when they are ill or nervous or dizzy. These animals do it when they feel fine. Some of them need to do it or they won't feel fine.

Some **frogs** hurl their babies into the world. *Barf them out?* Yep, their children spew forth into life.

The Australian brooding frog lives in only one country. Guess where. After a male frog fertilizes her eggs, the mother frog swallows up to 20 eggs. The eggs go into her stomach, but she doesn't digest. To stop the eggs from becoming froggie omelets, the mother's stomach stops making stomach acids. Also, she doesn't eat for the five weeks that the baby froglets develop. The eggs become complete little frogs, not tadpoles. After five weeks, the mother frog spits up wee froggies. I guess she doesn't care much for frog's legs.

ribit
ribit
croak
raaaaallllph!

"Got a frog in your throat?"
"Yep, several dozen to be exact."

Male Darwin's frogs may have frogs in their throats. Literally. The male frogs attract the female frogs by singing. OK, to humans it may sound more like croaking, but the female Darwin's frogs must find it romantic. The frogs meet—love at first sight —and mate. After they mate, the female frog takes off. No mothering instinct here. But the male frog hangs around and watches over the eggs. The father frog gathers up the eggs before they hatch. Only he collects them by swallowing. The trick is that he doesn't gulp the eggs into his stomach. Instead, he stores them in his vocal sac. No more singing for a while, as the eggs develop into tiny frogs. When the time is right, the new frogs are then barfed (or is it belched?) into the world.

Charles Darwin was a great natural scientist, who studied animals to help him form the theory of evolution. He found an odd male frog in Chile. It was later named after him.

YOU'RE AT YOUR GRANDMA'S HOUSE, CRAWLING ABOUT ON THE FLOOR, WHILE HER CAT LOUNGES NEARBY.
ON THE CARPET, YOU DISCOVER A WET MINI HOT DOG.

You inspect more closely; it's a hairy, damp hot dog. Then, suddenly from the couch, "Retch." Kitty hurls a lovely, warm, hairy hot dog. Aw, how sweet. A fresh hairball just for you. Now you can start a hairball collection of your very own.

If you really want to be disgusting, or if you are very curious, you can dissect the hairball. Pulling it apart will show that is mostly made of—guess what?—hair. Cats don't go around eating wads of hair but they do swallow hair when they groom themselves. Their scratching tongues make natural combs. The problem is that their stomachs cannot digest the hair. The hair there forms clumps. The hair wads only have two ways to get out.

Barfing or pooping.

Pooping them out can be difficult because the gut, or intestine, is very curvy. The hairy clump might get stuck. Not good because now kitty can't dookie. The meow doctor may give kitty a **laxative** **(LACKS a tiv)**, or poop-making medicine. If that doesn't work, shoving medicine up her butt or operating on her may work.

Nope, the poo route just doesn't work.

Combing kitty is the best. Cats shed fur during season changes and during stressful times. Cats lick their fur to remove the loose hair. If you comb kitty, he can lick away and not swallow hair. No more hairballs.

Another solution is hairball medicine, available in most pet stores. Hairball cures are usually flavored mineral oil or petroleum jelly. It's much cheaper to just smear a little petroleum on kitty's paws, or to add to kitty's din-din one teaspoon of mineral oil for each 10 pounds of cat. Do this once or twice week and kitty will be fine.

Unless, of course, you really want a hairball collection.

Cats may upchuck balls of their own hair, but owls actually hurl balls of fur from other animals.

No, the owls do not collect the hair by grooming other animals. They gather the hairy vomit by eating whole animals.

Owls are amazing eaters.

One bird researcher fed a barn owl nine mice in a row before the owl was full. Then, only three hours later, it topped off the nine-mouse meal with three more!

Owls are expert hunters, but when it comes to eating, their table manners probably would not be acceptable in most restaurants. After an owl captures dinner, such as a mole or a rat, it turns the animal around and swallows the whole thing head first.

The owl would probably chew dinner, except it has no teeth. Several hours later, the owl spews a bundle of fur, feather, teeth, claws, and bones called an **owl pellet**. And to make matters worse, the rude puker just lets the barf bag fly through the air and land. Talk about a projectile barf.

The pellets lie on the ground to become food and home for clothes moths, carpet beetles, and mold. For the clothes moth, the hair barf also serves as a nursery, as eggs are laid in the pellet. The moth caterpillars make cocoons with the leftover fur in the pellet. From the hairy cocoon new clothes moths form.

Sometimes the pellets don't stay on the ground for very long. Humans collect them.

WHY WOULD ANYONE WANT TO COLLECT OWL VOMIT PACKS? YUCK!

Owl pellets are actually pretty interesting. The owl's stomach breaks down the animal parts it can use, then it gathers the other parts into a pellet. Since the owl eats only whole food, the skeletons from entire animals lie hidden in the spewed packet. An average two-inch pellet contains the skeletons of three animals. People dissect the pellets to check out what's inside. The digestive juices in the owl's stomach stripped the meat from the bones. The clean bones can be arranged and glued to make a skeleton picture or a free-standing skeleton. Pellet-collecting scientists study the bones to find out what owls eat, and to learn about populations of small animals. So, the cast-off barf of the owl serves as human entertainment and information.

Who's the strange one—the owl or the human?

Owls can't move their eyes, but they can turn their heads in an almost complete circle. Do you think they can spew while spinning their heads? What a great trick that would be! Sign them up for horror films.

One bird researcher dissected 200 pellets from one owl. In the pellets he found:

412 mice

20 shrews

1 mole

1 sparrow

20 rats

OWL PELLETS

What you need: An owl pellet (you can collect pellets yourself or you can purchase owl pellet kits at some educational toy stores), sheet of white paper, tweezers, skewer or long needle, and glue.

What you do: Place the pellet onto the sheet of paper. Use the tweezers and skewer to tease the fur away from the bones. Collect the bones in a pile. Sort the bones into skulls, backbones, legs, etc. Figure out how many animals were in the pellet. Choose the bones that you think belong to one animal. Piece the bones to form a skeleton. Glue the skeleton together or glue the skeleton onto cardboard. Throw away the fur and other animal parts that you don't use.

Blood Slurpers

THE NEXT TIME YOU CRAVE A TREAT, TRY WHIPPING UP THIS RECIPE:

BLOOD SOUP

Drain the blood from one duck into a pan.
Add to it some duck meat, parsley, celery, onion, and dried prunes.
Boil it up and serve.

It's blood soup!

Want some?

OK,

so blood soup is not your cup of tea— or rather your cup of blood. But it is eaten with gusto by many Polish people.

Maybe this delicious snack will excite your taste buds: find a live ox, slice a small cut in the ox's vein, collect a gourd of blood, add fresh milk, agitate. Wha La! A blood milk shake. Drink and enjoy.

So a blood shake eaten by the Masai people of Africa doesn't thrill you either? How about a big beef steak, rare and bloody?

Is your mouth watering yet?

Most people wouldn't place humans in the blood-eaters category.

This is probably accurate, as most people would prefer to munch on French fries dipped in ketchup rather than blood.

However, yummy blood is the preferred meal for many animals, including lice, bedbugs, leeches, ticks, and mosquitoes. Imagine how restaurant menus would read if leeches chose to dine out. "Oh, I just don't know what to have. Human blood, fish blood, or maybe crocodile blood. It all sounds so yummy."

Being a blood eater is a pretty great thing because almost every creature has blood. And blood is very nutritious. Like peanut butter, blood contains lots of **protein (PRO teen)**. Protein is important for a healthy diet. Another important blood ingredient is metal. Metal like cars are made from? Yep, in humans and many other critters, the metal is iron. The same metal iron used to make cannons and frying pans. There's only a teeny tiny amount in blood so that living things don't become loaded down from carrying around their blood.

When iron meets oxygen gas, it makes red rust. The oxygen combining with the iron in blood makes it red. Although you think of the color red for blood, it also comes in clear and blue.

Have you ever seen a copper bracelet rust to a lovely blue color? Copper metal gives some animals stylish blue blood. Lobsters, crabs, pillbugs, shrimps, many spiders, and some snails and slugs have blue blood.

Clear blood means there is no metal in it. Insects have see-through blood. Besides protein and metal, blood is mostly salt water. So, blood contains water, salts, proteins, and metals. Just what the blood eaters ordered.

Cockroach blood is white.

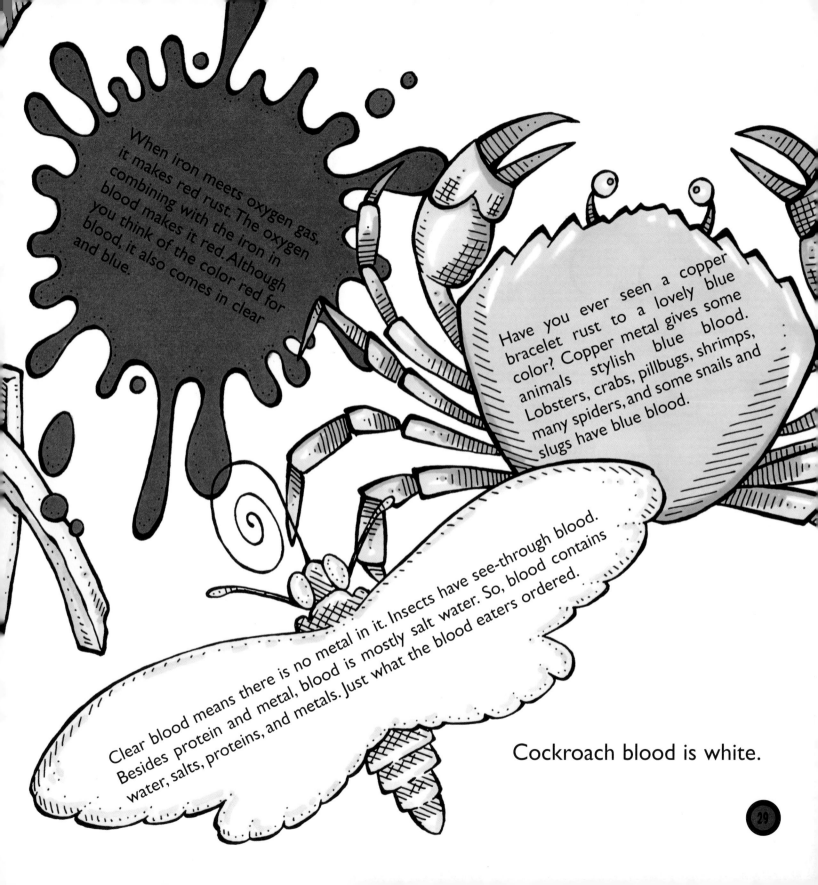

It heals bruises; sucks them away.

After major operations, it reduces swelling by sipping out the excess blood. Someday its spit may be used to treat tumors and other ailments.

Name that creature.

If you said the bloodsucker, or leech, you're right. If you said, **"Yuck! How disgusting,"** you are probably right, too.

At least until you get to know one.

Bloodsucker is the perfect name for this worm, because that's exactly what it does. Suck blood. Leeches can suck nine times their weight during one blood meal. This isn't so bad for most common bloodsuckers, which are about an inch long. But the giant leeches can be almost length of your arm.

"Whoa! Get it off!"

LEECH © Doug Wechsler/Animals Animals

Even electric eels can't stop a leech from eating. Several thousand leeches have been removed from a single electric eel.

How shocking!

Bloodthirsty leeches have two suckers. One is on the rear end. That is where the leech attaches to its live dinner. Also in the center of this sucker is the leech butthole. The other sucker is at the front end. That one contains razor-sharp teeth. The leech slices the skin with the teeth, injects saliva, or spit, into the area to lower the pain and to keep the blood flowing, then sucks blood with powerful throat muscles. One feeding may last for several hours. As it gorges, the slender worm-like body bloats. After it's full, the blood-filled creature drops off and waits several months, until it feels hungry again.

Left behind is the telltale sign of a leech attack—a Y-shaped cut.

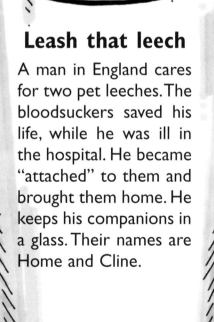

Leash that leech

A man in England cares for two pet leeches. The bloodsuckers saved his life, while he was ill in the hospital. He became "attached" to them and brought them home. He keeps his companions in a glass. Their names are Home and Cline.

31

The word **leech** may make your skin crawl, or it may make you think of a person you know. People who take advantage of others are often referred to as leeches.

However, **leech** is actually an old English word for **physician**. For centuries, leeches were used for blood letting. It was thought that leeches cured a person by sucking out the bad blood. In 1846, leeches became so popular that 20 to 30 million were used in France alone. During that time, a leech farm in the United States boasted of selling an average of 1,000 bloodsuckers every day. Leechcraft almost wiped out the sucking worms. Leeches are again gaining popularity for use in some operations.

WHO KNOWS?

You may avoid leech-filled waters and marshes, only to wake up one day in a clean, crisp hospital bed to find a leech sucking your blood.

Just when you thought it was safe to get in the leech-free water, the candiru fish arrives.

This little beast, only an inch long and toothpick-thin, has a very gruesome habit. It swims up the breathing gills of fishes to feast on their fresh blood.

No problem. I'm not a fish.
Yes, problem.

If you bathe or pee in candiru-filled water, the fish might confuse your body openings for a fish gill slit. The little menace travels up into your body parts. Usually it swims up the pee pee tube, attaches with barbs on its head, then sucks your blood. The little pointed head makes it impossible to pull out. Surgery is the only way to get rid of it.

"Excuse me, doctor, I was peeing in the water and I took on a little friend."

Actually, you need not worry much about meeting a candiru. They live only in the Orinoco and Amazon Rivers of South America.

Now you tell me!

TIC, TIC, TIC, TICK.

From a deep sleep, you awaken suddenly with a pain in your side. You touch the sore and feel a small hard spot. "Funny, a scab. I don't remember placing push pins in my bed."

You enter the bathroom to inspect the new wound at the mirror. When you touch the dark spot, it moves. "Ack! It's not a scab at all. It's a tick!" Shudder. Cringe. Uck. You seize the tweezers, grab the little body and pull. Out comes the crunchy critter. Upon close inspection, you realize only the body and the legs wriggle in the tweezers. The head remains embedded in your side! Help! Guess you'll have to dig it out.

Immediately, you feel another creeping crawly. It is probably your imagination. But then again, if the first biting tick is female, there just might be a little male climbing nearby.

Ticks are pretty high on the icky list. (Although a tick probably wouldn't think so.) Ticks eat only three times in their two-year-long life. Each is a blood meal from a warm-blooded animal. The baby tick hatches with a few brothers and sisters—about four or five thousand. The newborn tick, or larva, climbs on a grass blade and patiently waits for its first meal. Very patiently, as it may take several months for a mouse or a bird to stroll by.

TICKS © James H. Robinson/Photo Researchers, Inc.

The larva (with maybe several hundred of its brothers and sisters) scuttles onto breakfast, shoves its snout and harpoon-like mouth under the skin, attaches with its sticky spit, and starts sucking. As it "pigs out," the tick's belly gets bigger and bigger and BIGGER. The leathery underside stretches like a giant blood balloon. The tick's size increases several times just from its belly extending with blood.

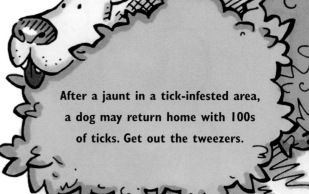

After a jaunt in a tick-infested area, a dog may return home with 100s of ticks. Get out the tweezers.

After several days of eating (talk about an eatfest), the tick pulls out its head and drops off. For the next few months, the baby tick digests its first meal, grows another pair of legs so it has a total of eight, and becomes a teenage tick, or a **nymph (NIMF)**. Then it decides to do lunch.

Again it waits, trying to detect the carbon dioxide from the breath of passing blood or a type of chemical called **butyric (byoo TEER ick)** acid released from lunch's skin. Lunch arrives. Again it climbs on. Again it gorges itself and drops off. The teen tick digests, turns into an adult, and moves onto a bush or low tree.

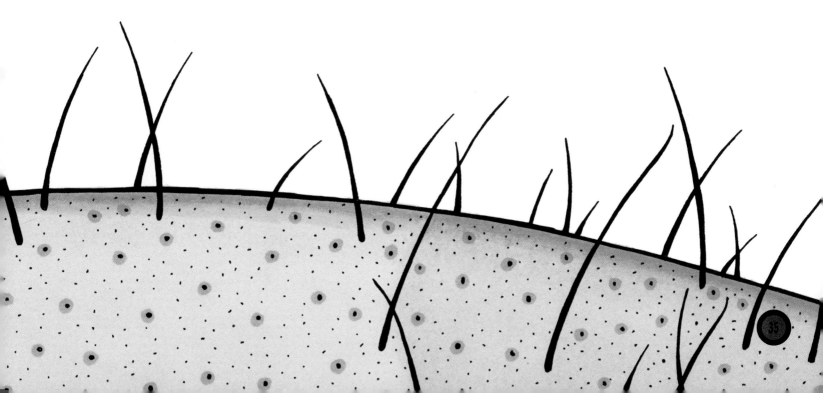

Ticks often relocate by hitching a ride on a migrating bird.

Then, guess what: dinner. This time it's usually a much bigger meal, like a dog, deer, or you. Only the female ticks are interested in dinner; the males have something else on their minds. After she digs in her head, the male reproduces with her. He then drops off and dies. She finishes her meal, drops off, lays eggs, and dies. That's it.

For a tick, it's be born, suck blood, grow, suck blood, grow some more, suck blood, reproduce, die. No parties or picnics, no cookies or oranges.

Hey, ticks don't really seem so bad. Ticks really aren't evil. Ticks earned a bad reputation because some ticks have very itsy bitsy critters inside their guts that cause dangerous diseases—not for the ticks, but for the animals they feed on. **Lyme (LIME) Disease** and **Rocky Mountain Spotted Fever** are two very serious and sometimes fatal illness caused by these wee beasties. To avoid the disease, you must avoid the innocent tick.

Here are several methods of tick control:

- **Remove a tick by slowly pulling the body with tweezers. If you yank, the head may stay behind.**

- **Keep your eyes on any tick bite to make sure a ring does not develop around the bite. If a ring develops, go to the doctor.**

- **When heading out into nature, wear pants tucked into boots or apply tick spray or pennyroyal oil.**

- **After returning from nature, check yourself and your pets for ticks. The longer the tick stays attached, the higher the chance of getting a disease.**

"GIRLS HAVE COOTIES. STAY AWAY FROM THEM."

This playground advice actually has some truth to it. Girls are more likely to have cooties than boys. A study conducted by the Center for Disease Control discovered that 10 percent of girls have cooties, compared with 7 percent of boys. And they're contagious!

What a lousy deal.

Exactly right. **Cooties** are a nickname for the blood-sucking **louse**.

Humans are everything to a louse—home, food, toilet, and graveyard. "I can't live without you." A louse can survive only several days without a human, and more than lifestyle attaches a louse to humans. The legs of this six-legged insect are equipped with gripping claws. The claws allow the louse to hang onto human hair. Neither rain nor winds nor a brush can get them off.

Lice (**Lice?** I thought it was **louse**. Like **mouse** and **mice**, more than one **louse** is called **lice**) come in three flavorful varieties. Take your pick. Head lice scuttle about the hairs of the scalp. Some may move to the suburbs—eyebrows and beards. Head lice are regaining popularity among school children. Crab or pubic lice prefer the coarse hair of armpits and UhUmmmmmm . . . more private parts. Body lice are more free. They live in clothing and bedding, biting any convenient skin.

Lousy History

Before he became a saint, Thomas à Becket was an English archbishop during the twelfth century. He wore a shirt made of hair that he refused to take off. After Thomas was murdered at Canterbury Cathedral, his shirt was found to be alive with body lice scurrying to find a new home.

During World War One, an army experiment supplied soldiers with cootie-proof underwear. The treated shorts didn't work very well.

Entire Native American villages overrun with lice would up and move, leaving their clothing and bedding behind.

No matter which variety you prefer, lice choose you. They don't have wings, so they can't fly. Lice crawl, pulling their large back end with six hooked legs from person to person. If you want lice, all you need to do is find a lousy person. (Besides meaning repulsive and inferior, **lousy** means infected with lice.)

To get body lice, sleep in the lousy person's bed, or borrow some clothing. For pubic lice, you need to get close, very close. Head lice are the easiest to obtain. Share a hat, swap combs, or hug. Your new pests, I mean pets, settle in quickly. No need to buy pet food. They just use their little lances to poke you and suck blood when hungry. Much easier than owning a dog or cat. When you begin to itch and scratch, you know they are happy.

And when they're happy, they reproduce, right on your body. How creepy. A female head louse can lay up to six eggs daily. She glues each egg to a hair shaft. The baby head lice hatch in about 10 days, feed, and begin to reproduce. After about a month, your head will be the proud owner of one very big, happy family.

The tiny silver eggs that mother lice stick to hairs are called nits. Before chemical treatments were around, nits were removed by picking through each strand of hair: thus the phrase nit picky for people who are very fussy.

At Zervas Elementary School in Massachusetts, a group of parents formed a special group—Nit Pickers. They wear t-shirts that read "Nit Picker—It's a Lousy Job," as they probe the students' heads for lice.

Itch.
Scratch.

"Ack!
**A louse farm I
am not. Get rid
of them."**

Picky, picky, picky. That's one
sure way to wipe them out. The
other way is to use louse treatment
kits, available at most drug stores. These treatments smell
really awful. However, the choice is somewhat limited:
itch, pick, or stink. Clothing and bedding
should also be cleaned.

**If you get lice, just remember
that it's not always nice to share.**

"Sleep tight and don't let the **bedbugs** bite." *Yeah right. Bugs in beds. I don't think so.* Think again. They even have an official name—**bedbugs**. **How descriptive.**

Actually, bedbugs hide in furniture and other cracks and crevices, usually in filthy places, like seedy motel rooms. After nightfall, when all is quiet, they become active. They hunt in the dark. Their prey: blood, human blood. At the smell of yummy human blood, the bugs give out little "Yips" of happiness. Only you don't hear the cheers because you are asleep. The bloodthirsty creatures scurry toward your slumbering body. They poke you with their long, beaklike mouths, then suck your blood using muscles in their heads.

You awaken with an "Ouch! What was that?" Then, just as you're dozing off, another attack. Only this time it's from the bedbug's cousin. The bug from the first bite is already hiding. The bites continue all night long. And you don't sleep tight. When you flip on the light after an attack, you see reddish-brown, six-legged beasts about a quarter of an inch long (that's about the width of a pencil). The bugs hate light and they race under the sheets to hide. You jump from the bed, pack your bags, and move to another motel.

So, sleep tight and don't let the bedbugs or lice or candiru or leeches or ticks bite.

FAKE BLOOD

What you need: Cornstarch, red food coloring, powdered cocoa, clear syrup (used for cooking not for pancakes), water, bowl, spoon, toothpick.

What you do: In the bowl, place 2 spoonfuls of syrup and 1 spoonful of water. Stir with the toothpick. Add 2 drops of red food coloring. Stir. To the mixture, add 2 pinches of cornstarch and 1 pinch of powdered cocoa. Stir well. Drip the blood from your mouth. Or better yet, put some in your mouth. (It is not harmful, but it doesn't taste too great.) Go find an unsuspecting person, then say, "I want to suck your blood."

Bedbug remains have been uncovered in Stone Age caves and Egyptian tombs.

Bedbugs have a worse enemy than humans. The assassin bug waits until a bedbug gorges on a blood meal. The assassin bug then charges, shoves its mouth into the bedbug's belly, and sucks out the secondhand blood meal.

Slime Makers

Sometimes people can be pretty slimy. No, not slimy like the kid who cons small children out of their lunch money. Really slimy, like the toddler with an unwiped snotty nose, or your sweaty neighbor returning from a jog in the summer heat. If you turned a human body inside out, you would find a lot of slime. That's because many glands in the human body produce **mucus (MEW cuss)**. Sticky, slippery, liquidy mucus slimes the nose, the throat, the stomach, and the intestines. Mucus helps to trap stuff, move stuff, and protect stuff. It's pretty good stuff.

Actually, most inside-out animals would be slimy. The great chemical, mucus, covers animal insides the world over.

Life would be very rough without mucus. Some animals produce mucus not just on the inside, but on the outside, too. The **hagfish** is just such an animal.

Cute, a **hagfish** is not. Actually, the name **hagfish** tells you that it wouldn't make a fond addition to a stuffed animal collection. This slime-making, gooey creature is a primitive fish. It has a worm-shaped body without any bones. Some hagfish can grow three feet long. Its tiny little eyes don't see very well. A hagfish mouth has hagfish lips that are used for sucking. Inside the mouth is a single tooth. Around the sucking mouth are several stubby whiskers, or **tentacles (TENT a culls)**. The slimy hagfish skin is grayish or brownish. Yep, a face and body that only a hagfish mother could love. The hagfish may be the slimiest creature on Earth.

Hagfish have earned the nicknames **slime hags** and **slime eels** because of their amazing oozing bodies. If you place a hagfish in a bucket of sea water, this animal drips so much slime that a thick layer of mucus will float on the water after several hours.

"Slime bucket," in this case, is not an exaggeration.

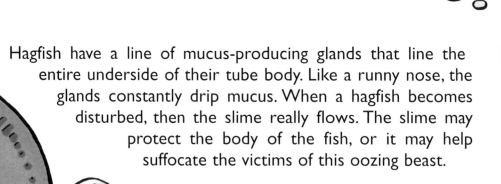

Hagfish have a line of mucus-producing glands that line the entire underside of their tube body. Like a runny nose, the glands constantly drip mucus. When a hagfish becomes disturbed, then the slime really flows. The slime may protect the body of the fish, or it may help suffocate the victims of this oozing beast.

A hagfish has not two, not three, but four hearts.

Each heart beats in a different rhythm.

Hagfish slime is not only skin deep. The lifestyle of this creature is a bit slimy, too. Since hagfish have just a tail fin, they don't swim very well. Mostly they slither around in the ocean muck. When a hagfish finds a sickly or dead fish, its sucking lips attach to the fish's gills, eyeball, or anus. Anus? Yep, butthole. Then it bores through with its single tooth and begins to suck. The hagfish slurps up the fishy insides through the opening. A hagfish single nostril leads right to its throat so the beast can smell as its head burrows deep into the victim. The meal is finished when only the skin and bones of the helpless fish are left. The hagfish lets go of the fish carcass and returns to the mud to wait for another meal.

One type of hagfish can eat up to 18 times its weight in only seven hours! A hagfish is not the animal you would choose to add to your aquarium.

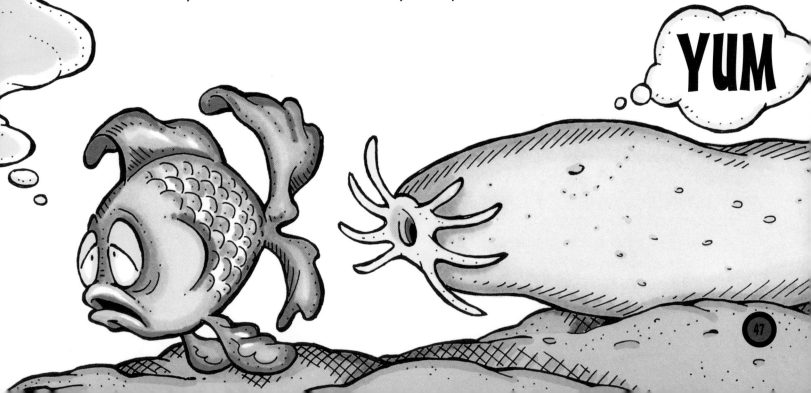

A close relative of the hagfish is the **lamprey (LAMB pree)**. Disgusting features must run in the family, as the lamprey looks very similar to the hagfish. The big differences are that the lamprey is not as slimy, and that it has two fins along its back, no tentacles, and a scarier mouth. The lamprey mouth is very round. The inside is loaded with razor teeth and a sharp tongue that also bears teeth. Unlike the hagfish, the lamprey chooses healthy creatures to feed upon.

When a fish or even a swimmer with cold legs comes near a lamprey, it attacks and attaches. The sucking lips close upon the skin of the victim. The sharp teeth gnaw through the surface. The special spit, or saliva, stops the prey's blood from clotting. Then the toothed tongue goes into action, lapping the blood of the captive. Lick, ouch, lick, ouch. Once full, the lamprey lets go. The victim doesn't die from the bite itself, but it bears a wound that may become infected. Infected lamprey bites cause the death of many fish in the ocean and in the Great Lakes. The rare human victim has never died from the attack. It's just a bit unnerving and uncomfortable to have an eel-like creature hooked to your leg.

So which is more putrid: a slimy, gut-sucking hagfish, or a sharp-tongued, blood-sucking lamprey? Guess it comes down to a matter of personal taste.

You awaken on a summer morning, after a rainy spring. Fling open the front door. Step barefoot onto the porch. **EeuwWW!**

You step into a greasy yellow blob. You gaze on the front yard and notice many oozy, crawling creatures. An alien life form! You grab the garden hose and blast the closest, slimy, Jell-O-like glob. It breaks apart into pieces. Ack, each piece has a life of its own! Now each part blobs about on your lawn. Help! It's the attack of the **slime mold**! You fall on the ground in frozen terror. The slime mold inches forward to devour you bit by bit.

Hey, I thought this was a true book. Well, the above story is true. At least until you get to the part about falling on the ground and being eaten by the slime mold. Slime molds are real. Really. They aren't alien creatures from outer space. They are . . .well, they're not animals, or plants, or molds. Slime molds belong to a special group of living things called **Protoctista**.

Isn't this book called Animal Grossology? Yeah, but slime molds are pretty slimy. Anyway, there aren't many books about Protoctista.

Slime molds can actually cover people's lawns and porches. In 1973, residents in suburbs near Dallas and near Boston panicked when slime molds tried to overtake their neighborhoods.

OK, slime molds actually don't crawl very fast. But they can move about as quickly as a slug. And OK, slime molds don't actually attack, but they do eat bacteria and other teeny tiny creatures.

A slime is a huge single cell. Cells are the building blocks of all living things. Your body has about 7,000,000,000 (7 trillion) living cells, or more cells than there are people, dogs, and cats living on the Earth. A slime mold has only one cell. This single cell may grow as large as the palm of your hand and a few may even get as large as a beach towel. Now that's a big cell. If the big cell breaks apart into smaller pieces, each part can become a new cell.

You probably wouldn't ask for a cuddly slime mold for your birthday, but slime molds can make great pets. They don't roll over or purr. They do slime around and some are very colorful. In the early 1900s, a man named Kumagusu kept pet slime molds in his garden. When he found out that garden slugs were feeding on his dear pets, he trained cats to act as mold guards.

Another slime-mold lover was Ruth Nauss. She kept her pets in jars and dishes in the living room. She took some of them on vacation with her. Hot water bottles warmed her pets on cold nights. One slimy pet lived for over nine years. If you decide a slime mold is the perfect pet for your bedroom, follow the activity directions for collecting and caring for slime molds.

Nope, you can't buy them at the local pet store.

An old horror film called *The Blob* featured a giant oozing creature that could creep about. The monster was similar to an overgrown slime mold with an attitude.

The largest slime mold ever recorded was 3 feet wide and 30 feet long. Imagine a slime mold covering the entire aisle of a bus. **Squish, Squish.**

PET SLIME MOLDS

What you need: A place to collect slime molds (swamps or moist woods are best), damp paper towel in a plastic bag, large bowl-shaped coffee filter, small bowl, water, ground-up oatmeal, large jar with a lid or a plate to cover the opening, and paper towels.

What you do: Look under rotting logs, fallen leaves, and dead twigs for a slimy blob. When you find a slime mold, introduce yourself, then place your new pet into the plastic bag. You need not remove your friend from its leaf or decaying wood. Take your new pet home. Prepare a slime mold house. Wrap the coffee filter around the small bowl to make a drum. Place the small bowl with the filter paper into the large jar. Make sure the filter paper is flat on the top of the bowl. Pour water down the side of the large jar. Add water until it just touches the bottom edge of the coffee filter. Place your new pet onto the flat top of the coffee filter drum. Feed your slime mold a pinch of ground oatmeal. Cover the jar loosely to keep out flies. Feed your slimy pet every day or two. Water when necessary. When it spreads to cover the filter paper, line the jar with paper towels. If your slime mold is happy, it will ooze over the water moat and onto the paper towels. Love your slime mold and don't forget to name it.

Pet Slime Molds

Water Level

NOPE, IT'S NOT A FRUIT THAT LIVES IN SALT WATER. A **SEA CUCUMBER** IS AN ACTUAL MARINE ANIMAL.

Let's get right down to the gooey details on sea cucumbers. Sea cucumbers are like giant bloated buns with oozing tentacles. The tentacle mucus helps to trap food for the creature. Sand eaters may pick up one grain at a time to suck on; these animals must eat almost nonstop day and night to get enough food. A muck eater swallows and poops out about 100 pounds of mud yearly.

Interesting, but not too gross or even slimy. Well, that's not all the slime on sea cucumbers. Some sea cucumbers have slimy, leathery skin. The poisonous slime keeps fish from chewing on the sluggish ocean blobs. But it does not keep people from eating sea cucumbers.

Yuck!

Sea cucumber food is called **trepang (tra PANG)**. Trepang is mostly eaten in Asian countries. The sea cucumbers are caught, sliced open, boiled, then dried in the sun. The dried stuff is usually made into a slimy, thick soup. Yummy for the tummy.

Again, interesting, but not too gross or even slimy.

OK, how's this for gross?
When a sea cucumber is really scared, it shoves its guts out of its butthole.
Now we're getting somewhere.

The sticky, slimy intestines and stomach entangle an attacker, or they just crawl around outside of the body for awhile. Some types of sea cucumber blow their guts out their butts each year during a specific season. No one is sure why. After it blows the slimy wad, the sea cucumber body crawls away and grows a whole new inside. This can take anywhere from nine days to several months.

And there's more slimy butt stuff from sea cucumbers. *Tell me.* When under threat, some sea cucumbers shoot long white or red threads from their anus, or buttholes. The threads are tough and covered in sticky mucus. The attacker becomes wound up in the swelling anal threads. The more it struggles, the longer the threads become. Of course, the sea cucumber doesn't hang around for the sticky affair. It creeps away; its butthole kept it safe.

Disgusting enough?

It'll do.

One kind of sea cucumber lives under the ocean mud. It digs a U-shaped home with two openings. The feeding tentacles stick out of one hole, while the butt sticks out the other. Another hole-digging sea cucumber digs only a single opening. This is because the mouth and anal opening are together. How convenient.

You have probably seen snails sliming along the grass.

Snails are pretty gross, with their giant, oozing, fleshy feet. Well, imagine a snail without a shell. More slime, more gooey, more disgusting—a fleshy blob of mucus. A snail without a shell is a **slug**.

Ever feel sluggish, or really lazy? Actually, the word **sluggish** comes from the slow-moving snail-without-a-shell animal. Slugs are harmless to humans, but they are so revolting that most people prefer to avoid touching one. Of course, there are exceptions. Some naturalists have been known to not only pick up the yucky creatures, but to kiss or lick them. After they find out that slug bodies are covered with tiny mites, the kiss fest usually ends.

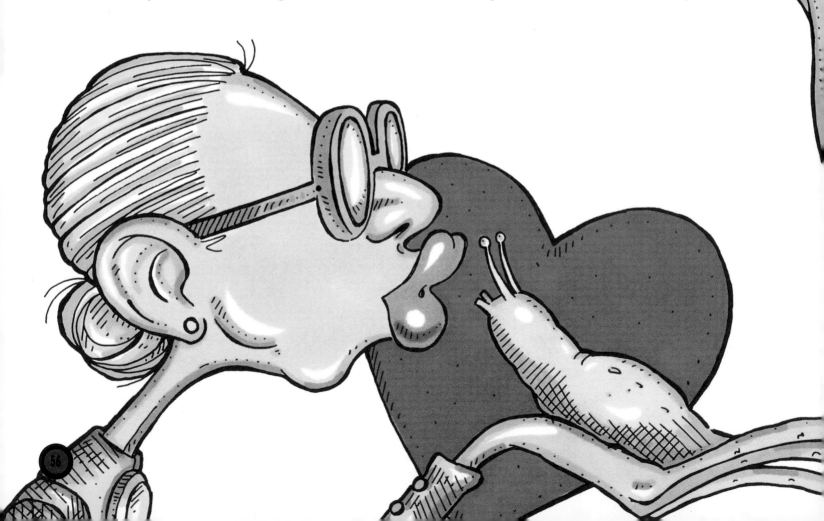

Slugs live both in the sea and on land. Land slugs are the slimiest because they need to protect their fleshy covering from drying out. They also gush slime from under their bodies to help them move about. The garden slug is small and looks like a gray-colored little finger. The banana slug looks like guess what? Yep, either a ripe yellow or a splotchy rotten fruit, and it's about the same size, as well. The largest land slug is the European slug, which grows to a foot long. And the bigger the slug, the more the slime.

The entire life of a slug is gushy. Baby slugs begin their oozy life by hatching from gelatin eggs. From then on, it's slither and gush. Mucus oozes from all over the body. A gland on the bottom near the front end of the creature squirts out thick, sticky mucus. The slug travels on this constant highway of slime. The layer of slime is great because a slug can travel over thorns, nails, and rocks without getting hurt. The mucus and the foot together create a suction. This enables slugs to climb up things such as plant stalks and trees.

Yes, a tree-climbing slug.

Some slugs can make a cord from a special mucus spot in their tail end. The slime cord acts like a rope to lower a slug to the ground from a high place. Imagine bumping into a slug hanging in space from a clear mucous rope. A real slug in the face that would be.

If a slug is attacked, it humps up its body and gobs on the slime. For some animals, the tasty morsel is now too big and slippery to eat. Other attackers can't stand the feel of the slime. As they try to unslime themselves, the slug makes a slow getaway. For other animals, the slime is too nasty to eat.

Yucky!

However, some animals, such as snakes, salamanders, and other slugs, don't seem to mind the slimy taste. Although you won't find slugs on a restaurant menu, people have stomached this creature. Northern California native peoples ate slugs, but only when food was hard to find. Also, German immigrants ate slugs after gutting them, removing the slime with vinegar, then deep frying them. Who knows? It could be a taste treat.

A slug cleans itself by slipping out of its dirty slime coat. When the dirty slime layer reaches the tail, the slug bites off or eats the dirty laundry. In no time, a new shiny mucus coat is on. No need to lick, or preen, or wash, just ooze.

The banana slug is the school mascot for the University of California at Santa Cruz.

Even the mating practices of slugs is mushy. Mushy like a romantic movie? No, mushy like a rotten tomato. Slugs don't meet other slugs often, so every slug is both female and male. This is true for snails as well. When two slugs meet, they create a cozy blanket of goo. The slugs may then taste each other's slime. "Ooooh, I just love to slurp on your slime." At mating time, each slug fertilizes the other. After parting both slugs are pregnant.

The pregnant slugs go off and lay their gushy eggs to begin a whole new generation of slimy creatures.

"Over hill, over dale, we will slime each dusty trail. The slugs and snails keep oozing along."

SNAIL SLIME

What you need: Snail, clear plastic, pebbles or marbles or other small stuff, and lettuce.

What you do: Find a snail. Morning or evening is usually the best for snail hunting. Lift the snail gently by the shell. Place the snail on a sheet of clear plastic. Hold up the plastic to observe the snail as it crawls. If the snail won't move, place some lettuce at one end of the plastic. Place objects on the plastic. Watch the snail glide across the objects. Observe from above and below the snail. If you feel really brave, place the snail on your hand. Feel the creature slime across your palm. Return the animal to a moist area.

Dookie Lovers

Birdie, birdie in the sky,
Dropped some whitewash in my eye.
Gee, am I glad cows don't fly.

Yep, birds do it. Bees do it. Cows, elephants, and fleas do it. All living things do it. All living things make waste. They poop on the land, in the lakes, and in the oceans. Plants? Well, plant poo is not exactly like doggie doo. The waste from plants is the gas oxygen. We actually need to breathe in plant waste or we would die. Plant garbage is our fresh air.

Basically, you could say that everything comes from caca. The soil that grows our food is filled with earthworm and bug waste. Rich soil is dookie soil. Yep, poop is great poop.

Poo, poop, caca, number two, dookie, doo doo, stool, and **crap** are words that you may use to describe the bodily waste you come in contact with most often. Oh yeah, you may want to add **turd** to the list. When it comes to animals besides ourselves and our pets, other words are used.

Cow, elephant, and camel turds are described as **dung**, **pies**, **pat**, and **chips**. When you come across pile of this waste, the names seem very accurate. **Manure (ma NEW ur)** is used for farm animal waste. So, an elephant in the wild would plop **dung** or **chips**, but a tame elephant would deposit **manure**. For some reason, **manure** just seems so much more polite.

Wild animals, such as wolves and mountain lions, leave behind **scat**. So, in the kitty litter box, it's **poo poo**, but for a cougar it is scat. Funny it's the same word, **scat**, that people use to drive away a cat. **Droppings** or **pellets** refer to the little round poop balls made by deer, elk, and goats. The big droppings plopped by a horse are sometimes named **road apples** due to their large size.

Handy Dandy Butt Candy Name Chart

NAME	ANIMAL
poo, poop, caca, number two, dookie, crap, turd, stool	all animals including humans
dung, pies, pat, chips	large grazing animals—cows, camels, elephants
manure	farm animals
scat	wild animals—mountain lions, coyotes, wolves
pellets, droppings, round poops, road apples	deer, elk, rabbits, horses
droppings, splay	birds
guano	bats, seabirds
feces, excreta, dejecta	scientific names for any animal's dookie

People in rural Germany used to place their manure piles in their front yards! The larger the manure pile, the wealthier the people in the home.

Bird doo doo is called **droppings**, as well. Probably because it is squirted from a great height, and then drops into a splat. A more accurate term for bird droppings is **splay**. When you think about the sound of bird dookie hitting a car window, **splay** is definitely the right word.

Seabirds and bats have their own special poo poo name, **guano (GOO on oh)**. Usually these birds hang out in large groups at a particular spot and dookie away. The poop pile just grows. People collect the wonderful guano and use it for fertilizer.

To be really scientific about the whole thing, you use the words **feces (FEE sees)**, **excreta (X cree ta)**, and **dejecta (da JEK ta)**. If you found this entire discussion of proper caca terms too much to remember, you can refer to the handy dandy butt candy name chart. Never again will you be embarrassed by using the wrong word in proper company.

DOOKIE TAG

What you need: Several friends, outdoor playing area, and a list of dookie names.

What you do: This game is very similar to television tag. Find a playing area. Set boundaries. There is no free area. One person is the scatologist. The scatologist tries to tag the other players, the dookies. If a person is tagged, he or she has two seconds to call out a word for dookie. Once a type of dookie is named, that person is free until he or she is tagged again. The catch of the game is that each dookie name can be used only once. For example, if the word **scat** was called and another tagged person says **scat** again, that person is out of the game. It makes the game easier if one player acts as recorder to write down each of the names called out in the game. The game continues until only the scatologist and one player are left.

Scatologists study dookie. Yep, and you, too, can grow up to be a dookie expert.

You may think that if you've seen one turd, you've seen them all. But different animals make different caca. For starters, it is very easy to tell meat-eating animals from plant eaters. Carnivore dookie, or excreta from a carnivore, often contains hair, feathers, and bones. A sniff test is foul and disgusting. Droppings from an herbivore, or plant eater, may contain straw, plant parts, or berry pits. A sweet smell floats from the berry eaters. Animals that eat fish and other marine life emit dookie with a fishy odor.

Sniff. Sniff. Smell any fish?

Texture and shape are important for feces identification. You are probably familiar with dog and cat caca. Wild dog and cat turds look similar to your pet's poo. However, coyotes and cougars don't get canned kibbles, so their poop may contain fur and bones. The hairs hold the bowel mass together, making the individual poops longer than Fido's or Muffy's, and pointed at the end. The entire world is a kitty litter box for a mountain lion. If you see scratch marks on the ground and an attempt to cover the dump, it is probably the leavings of a wild cat.

Bird splay is actually a combination of pee and poop. The little bit of poo is located in the center of the soft mass. The white stuff around the outside is the urine. A bird body removes most of the water and salts from the pee before dropping it. The white stuff is uric acid. Human pee pee contains urea. The uric acid in bird pee is twice as concentrated as the urea in human urine.

A pile of little round turds tells you a rabbit, deer, moose, or elk left its calling card. Rabbit droppings are small and round. Moose and elk stools are larger, about the size of large marbles. Deer poops are a bit flattened and a darker brown. A pile of large round lumps with bits of grass are the sure sign of a horse.

It takes a special eye to tell the exact bird from its splay. However, a trained bird dookieologist can do just that. To tell a bird from its leavings, two characteristics play an important role. What makes up the fecal center in the whitewash, and how does the whitewash run?

Duck dookie has a lot of fecal matter, usually brown in color, but not much whitewash. Barn owl splays don't have feces. Owls barf out the fur and bones. This makes for clean cacaless droppings. Some beautiful starbust splays are deposited by the little chickadees.

Some people collect stamps, and others may collect coins. The collection of researcher Olaus Murie contains over 1,200 turd specimens. The poops are dried, varnished, mounted, and labeled.

Since so much bird dookie falls from the sky and from so many different types of birds, you could spend hours studying and reading books on this fascinating topic. Needless to say, the limited space in this book devoted to bird turds serves as only an introduction.

I'm glad.

Deer poop between 13 and 22 times every day.

Imagine if humans had to go that often.

Dogs are very well known for their dookie-eating games.

"No Fido, put that down!" Most dogs ignore their humans, munch on the tasty turd, then saunter over to their owners and lick, lick.

"Eeeuw."

Maybe humans are missing out. I DON'T THINK SO.

The scientific name for caca eating is **coprophagy (caw PRUF faj eee)**. This word comes from the Greek words **kopr-**, or dung, and **-phagos**, or eating. Seems like dookie munching has been around for a long time.

Some poops are more appealing to dogs than others. Turds with undigested food bits are the favorite. And once Rover develops a taste for pinched loaves, the habit is very difficult to break.

No one is really sure why dogs like to eat feces so much. Theories on coprophagy include boredom; an unbalanced diet; and lack of vitamins, minerals, or digestion chemicals. A doggie doctor who studied coprophagy concluded that dookie eating is just plain old normal for a dog.

Born to eat dookie.

Dogs greet each other by sniffing each other's butts. Actually, there's a good reason for this gross practice. Dogs have scent glands near their buttholes. The scent sacs help dogs to identify each other.

Sniff, sniff. "Oh, Buddy, it's you! I didn't recognize you at first."

Most poops probably wouldn't hurt your dog, but some feces may contain harmful germs and other small critters that could make your pet sick. Since Spot doesn't know any better, one of the following treatments may help change this habit.

- **Feed high-quality dry food with a bit of canned food mixed in.**
- **Add mineral and vitamin supplements to the food.**
- **Tell FiFi "No! Bad dog!" every time she nibbles on a turd.**
- **Sprinkle a little meat tenderizer on the food.**
- **Make your dog's dookie taste yucky by adding glutamic acid, carrots, pineapple, or pumpkin to his food.**
- **Clean up the doo doo before Rover gets to it.**

Some dog lovers have tried all of the above treatments, only to find that their beloved pet still enjoys a poo morsel every so often. If none of the treatments work on your pup, just don't let your dog lick you after a stool feast.

Tapeworms grow inside your stomach.

If you don't eat, they get really hungry and they flop around in your stomach to tell you it's feeding time. To get rid of tapeworms, you need to starve yourself for several days. Then you place a piece of meat on your tongue. The tapeworm is so hungry, it will climb up your throat and into your mouth to get the food. Then you just grab the worm and pull it out.

The old tapeworm story is not true. But don't worry, the real truth is still gross.

A tapeworm is a very lazy creature. Its head has hooks or suckers but no mouth, ears, or eyes. The head attaches to the inside of your intestine. The tapeworm just hangs out, seeps up nutrients from your food, and excretes inside your gut tube.

The only other thing a tapeworm does is reproduce. Each tapeworm segment has both male and female parts. When a section gets fertilized, the eggs develop. One segment can have up to 10,000 eggs. Now that's a lot of baby tapeworms. The pregnant section then drops off the tapeworm. One tapeworm can loose up to ten segments each day. Hey, that means 100,000 eggs! Yep, many tapeworms. When a person takes a dump, the eggy segments come out in the poops.

Tapeworms are long flat worms. Some can grow up to 60 feet long, or greater than the length of a large bus. Tapeworms have a round head and a ribbonlike body made of many segments. And they do live inside of humans. They don't live in a person's stomach; they live in a person's intestine, or gut tube. Humans have two intestines. The small intestine is about 20 feet long, connects to the stomach, and moves mushed up food. The large intestine is about five feet long and it turns the mushed up food into poop. A 60-foot-long tapeworm inside of a human must fold over many times. You could think of a tapeworm as being like a train. Each little segment is like a train car. As the tapeworm grows, it adds more cars to the front of train behind the head.

If the infected caca is eaten by another animal, the eggs develop in the muscles of the animal. The developing tapeworm is called a **worm bladder**. Each bladder contains the new head of a tapeworm. If the bladder-infected muscle is eaten by a human,

Wah la!, a tapeworm is born.

Common human tapeworms are beef tapeworms, pork tapeworms, broad fish tapeworms, and dwarf tapeworms. Beef, pork, and fish tapeworms come from eating infected meat that isn't cooked well. "I like my steak raw." "I just love sushi." Infected meat may look as though it has the measles. The pock marks are actually baby tapeworms. Beef, pork, and fish tapeworm is not common in places where meat is inspected before it can be sold. The dwarf tapeworm is less than an inch long. As with the other tapeworms, the eggs come out in human dookie. The eggs are spread by the person's butt-wiping hand.

Although a person with a tapeworm may lose a few pounds, the tapeworm also takes away much of the important nutrients in the person's food. This causes weakening, or anemia. Sometimes the tapeworm excreta can poison a person. If the tapeworm becomes too fat and happy, it will keep on growing. This can block the intestine, so that poops can't be released. Usually, a tapeworm just hangs out. In parts of Africa, tapeworms are so common that over half of the people in some villages carry one in their gut.

To get rid of tapeworms, doctors give medicines that kill the worm. The dead worm segments come out in the poops.

Awwww. I kinda like the raw-meat-on-the-tongue cure better.

TO SOME ANIMALS, DUNG IS THEIR ENTIRE LIFE.

An interview with a **dung beetle** would be pretty crappy. "I love dookie. I am born from dung. I eat it. I mold and shape it. My life is filled with doo doo." At the lovely smell of poofume, the dung beetles become excited.

"Yes, dung! Here I come."

The dung pile is so thrilling, it may attract dung beetles from all around. One seven-gallon elephant pie (seven-gallon dookie pile? Yep, elephants make major poops) may attract thousands of dung beetles looking for a fresh meal.

Yummmmmy.

Some types of dung beetles just eat their loaf when it's fresh and warm. One kind of dung beetle, the **scarab (SCARE ab)** beetle, is a real caca artist.

A scarab beetle doesn't just approach a newly laid pie and start chowing down. It begins by sorting through the pile. "Straw. Nope. Shovel it aside with my flat head. Worm eggs. Yuck. Push it away with my front arms. **Pure poo. Yes. Gather it up.**"

After a complete sorting, there is nothing but noncrap left behind. The beetle scoops poop armfuls under its belly and gives it a big dung beetle hug. "I love my dookie so." The magnificent bowed back legs begin to shape the caca glob. Turn, pat, pat, turn. The scarab adds more fresh poo to the ball until it's marble-sized. "Not big enough. I need more caca." Lemon-sized. "More. More." Apple-sized. "That's more like it." The poop art is now quite a bit larger than the beetle.

Making the giant round pat is just the first trick. The scarab beetle gets into position—head to the ground and back legs perched upon the excreta prize. It begins to roll. Really talented rollers can move their dung 15 yards a minute under perfect conditions. Roll, roll, roll the poo.

Most of the time the conditions are not perfect. Small hills may cause the doo doo ball and the beetle to fumble. "Up the hill. Down the hill." A scarab may falter with its prize several times before trying another route.

Also, dung ball stealers may attack. "Hey, there's a perfect poo ball. If I could just nab it, I wouldn't have to make one." Sometimes the ball stealers pretend to help out the working beetle. When the time is right, they try to make off with the ball. A dung beetle battle may arise. The doo doo nabber grabs the precious poo and holds on. The rightful owner climbs on top of the ball to stake its claim. The thief attempts to knock the beetle off of the dung log and climb on.

The battle of the ball rages until one beetle gives up.
Usually no major injuries are suffered.

If the scarab makes it over the hill and succeeds in fending off attackers, the ball is brought to a safe burial spot away from the dung insanity. The scarab releases its future poo ball treat to dig a hole. The ball is placed into the hole for many days of delightful nibbling.

A dung beetle prefers a caca ball any day over a cocoa ball.

Dung balls are more than meals for the beetles; they also serve as nurseries for new beetles.

The female dung beetle lays her egg in the ball. The baby dung beetle, or larva, looks like a fat worm. The larva eats its way out of the yummy dung nursery. For some types of dung beetles, only the females form and roll the dookie balls. Other types of dung beetles share the chore. The male makes the poopy nursery. "Oh! The nursery is just as I pictured it." The happy couple may share the ball rolling, with the male pushing and the female pulling. Or the female may ride the dung ball, scampering on top like a lumberjack in a log rolling contest. Only it's a much different kind of log for the dung lovers.

Dung beetles are great. *Everyone's entitled to their own opinion, I guess.* If it weren't for dung beetles, chips would pile up everywhere. A world buried in dung might result. Dung, dung, everywhere and not a spot to think.

The ancient Egyptians called the dung beetle the sacred scarab beetle. They believed the rolling of the dookie ball was symbolic of the force that rolled the sun across the sky.

OK, OK, dung beetles are necessary.

Yep, dung beetles are marvelous.

78

EDIBLE DOOKIE COOKIES

What you need: Measuring cups, measuring spoons, mixing bowl, cookie tray, sauce pan, oven, mixing spoon, margarine, cocoa, brown sugar, white sugar, vanilla, flour, rolled oats, shredded wheat or wheat flake cereal, and green food coloring.

What you do: Get an adult to warm the oven to 375°. Into the sauce pan place 1/2 cup margarine, 1/2 cup white sugar, and 4 teaspoons cocoa. Melt the mixture. Set aside. Into the mixing bowl add 1/2 cup brown sugar packed, 1 egg, 1/2 teaspoon vanilla, 1 cup flour, and 1 cup rolled oats. Stir well. Add the melted cocoa mixture. Stir well. Add a squirt of green food coloring and mix. Add the cereal and mix. (If you use shredded wheat, crumble the cereal first.) Shape the dough into turds. You can make flattened cow pies or little kitty turds. The cookie dough will flatten a bit during cooking, so keep that in mind. Place the cookies into the oven. Bake for 9–11 minutes. Remove. To serve, it looks best to place a single cookie on a plate or in a napkin. Find someone who didn't smell baking cookies and say,

"Hey, want a yummy treat?"

More Planet Dexter Books!!

THE HAIRY BOOK

The (Uncut) Truth About the Weirdness of Hair
by the Editors of Planet Dexter

Think you know hair? Think again! This hair-covered book gives you the real scoop on everything from blue-haired dogs to werewolves, wacky styles, and hairy babies. Includes a truly stylin' comb, for proper book grooming.

GROSSOLOGY

The Science of Really Gross Things!
by Sylvia Branzei

Yup, it's slimy, oozy, stinky, smelly stuff explained. *Grossology* features the gag-rageous science behind the body's most disgusting functions: burps, vomit, scabs, ear wax, you name it. Who could ask for anything more?

INSTANT CREATURE!

The Swimming Critters from Way Back Then!
by the Editors of Planet Dexter

Just add water to the little packets that come with *Instant Creature*, and you've got instant life. No joke! These aren't brine shrimp, and they aren't sea monkeys. What are they? Well, if we told you here, you wouldn't have to buy the book, would you?